I0828747

Rose Hartwick Thorpe.

RINGING BALLADS

INCLUDING

CURFEW MUST NOT RING TO-NIGHT

BY

ROSE HARTWICK THORPE

BOSTON
D LOTHROP COMPANY
FRANKLIN AND HAWLEY STREETS

PRESS OF HENRY H. CLARK & CO., BOSTON.

TO MY HUSBAND

THESE BALLADS

ARE AFFECTIONATELY DEDICATED

BY

THE AUTHOR.

Contents.

PAGE

Preface 11

Curfew Must Not Ring To-Night 17

Margaret 23

The Station Agent's Story 28

The Red Cross 35

Down the Track 44

In the Mining Town 47

In Answer 50

The Bridge of San Martin 53

Thanksgiving Day 58

The Soldier's Reprieve 62

The Luck of Muncaster 66

The Little Bells 72

Drinking Annie's Tears 77

A Brave Emperor 81

The Queen and the Beggar's Child 85

Love's Avowal 87

Lost at Sea 89

Kisses 91
Two Pictures 95
How the Flowers Came 99
Remember the Alamo 101
Historical Notes 111
The Last Night 114

ILLUSTRATIONS.

Portrait Rose Hartwick Thorpe . . . . *Front.*

PAGE

"With drowsy ripple, glint, and gleam,
The bending willows under" 13

"He with steps so slow and weary, she with sunny, floating hair" . . . 19

"O the sea! the stormy, tempestuous sea!" 25

"Each night and morn the torture of suspense and fear combine
To rob the aching head of rest, to fill the heart with pain" 39

The Bridge of San Martin 55

"Two thousand soldiers came in time
To stay the Douglas slaughter" 69

"The loveliest flowers on earth," he said,
"They bloom by a cottage wall" 75

"We are starving! bring us bread". 83

"Over lip and cheek and forehead
Like a shower caresses fall" 93

"Come you to worship at our shrine,
The shrine o' Texas Liberty?" 103

RINGING BALLADS

PREFACE.

Beside St. Joseph's shallow stream,
Whose crystal waters wander,
With drowsy ripple, glint, and gleam,
The bending willows under,

In the resplendent twilight hour,
When western skies were golden,
And solitude held magic power
With superstition olden,—

Just where the glory flushed the stream,
A shy-faced, sun-brown maiden,
Whose eyes had caught the sunset gleam,
Whose hands were blossom-laden,

Oft lingered there, wide boughs beneath,
The twilight hush around her,
To cull sweet flowers and weave a wreath,
Some day, perchance, to crown her.

PREFACE.

Her blossoms were those simple blooms
Which nature sometimes wedges,
In crowded places, mid the glooms
Of shady hazel hedges;

That push their heads above the sod,
In many a rude fence-corner,—
But still they were the flowers of God,
Fit jewels to adorn her.

Many a rose she wove, betimes,
Mid simple, wayside posies;
For love, so sweet and thorny, finds
Its counterpart in roses.

And still her garland grew and grew,
While summer skies were hazy,
With here and there a pansy blue,
And here and there a daisy,

And here and there a buttercup,
Plucked where the bees were humming;
For all her blossom-world looked up
And smiled to greet her coming.

Once, in a leafy, woodland bower
By girlhood's sunny portal,

WITH DROWSY RIPPLE, GLINT AND GLEAM,
THE BENDING WILLOWS UNDER.

PREFACE.

She found a sweeter, rarer flower,
That grew from seed immortal.

The great world said: "'Tis wondrous fair!
We do not want your posies;
But give to us this blossom rare,
This regal queen of roses."

She plucked it forth from bud and leaf
That clustered close about it,
She gave it—but her rosy wreath
Was incomplete without it.

The great world said: "'Tis wondrous fair!
Unlike your wayside posies.
Go thou, and find more blossoms rare,—
Bring us more queens of roses."

Her sweet hedgerows are left behind,
Long past is girlhood's portal;
Perchance she never more will find
Flowers grown from seed immortal.

But she has other rosy blooms,
Not quite devoid of graces,
Gleaned here and there among life's glooms
And in its sunny places.

PREFACE.

Accept the many for the one,—
The starry lights, God-given,
Are countless, while a single sun
Illumes the dome of heaven.

Some weary one along life's way,
Dazed by the sun's fierce splendor,
Would miss those starry eyes if they,
More brilliant, were less tender.

Sweet clover-bloom and cowslip fair,
Though field and meadow posies,
May still be loved, and honors share
With Love's bright queen of roses.

Curfew Must Not Ring To-Night.

ENGLAND'S sun was slowly setting o'er the hill-tops far away,
Filling all the land with beauty at the close of one sad day;
And its last rays kissed the forehead of a man and maiden fair, —
He with steps so slow and weary, she with sunny, floating hair:
He with bowed head, sad and thoughtful; she with lips so cold and white,
Struggled to keep back the murmur, "Curfew must not ring to-night!"

"Sexton," Bessie's white lips faltered, pointing to the prison old,
With its walls so tall and gloomy, — moss-grown walls dark, damp, and cold, —
"I've a lover in that prison, doomed this very night to die
At the ringing of the curfew, and no earthly help is nigh.
Cromwell will not come till sunset"; and her lips grew strangely white
As she spoke in husky whispers, "Curfew must not ring to-night!"

"Bessie," calmly spoke the sexton (every word pierced her young heart
Like a gleaming death-winged arrow, like a deadly poisoned dart),
"Long, long years I've rung the curfew from that gloomy, shadowed tower;
Every evening, just at sunset, it has tolled the twilight hour.
I have done my duty ever, tried to do it just and right;
Now I'm old I will not miss it: Curfew bell must ring to-night!"

Wild her eyes and pale her features, stern and white her thoughtful brow,
And within her heart's deep centre Bessie made a solemn vow.
She had listened while the judges read, without a tear or sigh,
"At the ringing of the curfew Basil Underwood *must die.*"
And her breath came fast and faster, and her eyes grew large and bright;
One low murmur, faintly spoken, "Curfew *must not* ring to-night!"

She with quick step bounded forward, sprang within the old church door,
Left the old man coming, slowly, paths he'd trod so oft before.
Not one moment paused the maiden, but, with cheek and brow aglow,
Staggered up the gloomy tower where the bell swung to and fro;
As she climbed the slimy ladder, on which fell no ray of light,
Upward still, her pale lips saying, "Curfew *shall not* ring to-night!"

"HE, WITH STEPS SO SLOW AND WEARY; SHE, WITH SUNNY FLOATING HAIR."

She has reached the topmost ladder; o'er her hangs the great, dark bell;
Awful is the gloom beneath her, like the pathway down to hell.
See, the ponderous tongue is swinging! 't is the hour of curfew now!
And the sight has chilled her bosom, stopped her breath and paled her brow.
Shall she let it ring? No, never! Her eyes flash with sudden light,
As she springs and grasps it firmly: "Curfew *shall not* ring to-night!"

Out she swung, far out; the city seemed a speck of light below,
There 'twixt heaven and earth suspended, as the bell swung to and fro.
And the sexton at the bell-rope, old and deaf, heard not the bell;
Sadly thought that twilight curfew rang young Basil's funeral knell.
Still the maiden, clinging firmly, quivering lip and fair face white,
Stilled her frightened heart's wild beating: "*Curfew shall not ring to-night!*"

It was o'er!—the bell ceased swaying, and the maiden stepped once more
Firmly on the damp old ladder, where, for hundred years before,
Human foot had not been planted. The brave deed that she had done
Should be told long ages after. As the rays of setting sun
Light the sky with golden beauty, aged sires, with heads of white,
Tell the children why the curfew did not ring that one sad night.

O'er the distant hills comes Cromwell. Bessie sees him, and her brow,
Lately white with sickening horror, has no anxious traces now.
At his feet she tells her story, shows her hands, all bruised and torn;
And her sweet young face, still haggard with the anguish it had worn,
Touched his heart with sudden pity, lit his eyes with misty light.
"Go! your lover lives," cried Cromwell. "Curfew shall not ring to-night!"

Wide they flung the massive portals, led the prisoner forth to die,
All his bright young life before him, 'neath the darkening English sky.
Bessie came, with flying footsteps, eyes aglow with lovelight sweet,
Kneeling on the turf beside him, laid his pardon at his feet.
In his brave, strong arms he clasped her, kissed the face upturned and white,
Whispered, "Darling, you have saved me! curfew will not ring to-night."

MARGARET.

FAIR Margaret! beautiful Margaret!
  In the hush of the twilight cold.
The sun on a dazzling throne has set
  In a cloud of amber and gold;
And the great green waves, with their white caps wet,
  O'er the beach to her feet have rolled.

She waits for the lover whose kiss one day
  Was pressed on her quivering lips,—
The lover who went from her side away
  In one of those swift-sailing ships,
O'er the waves that bright in the sunlight lay
  'Neath the glow of its finger-tips.

O the sea! the stormy, tempestuous sea!
  The sea with its roar and its gloom,—

The treacherous sea, how it shouts in glee
   O'er each jewel-decked coral tomb!
The glorious, grand, resplendent sea,
   In the light of a golden noon!

Whenever the shadowy twilight creeps
   O'er the earth, with her fair feet wet,—
When the stars come out and the great world sleeps,
   When the murmuring waters fret
On the sandy shore,—then she waits and weeps,
   Lonely, sorrowful Margaret!

There she sits alone mid the gleaming sands,
   By the shadowy ivied wall,
While over the clasp of her trembling hands
   Like a shower the tear-drops fall;
And the sea brings murmurs of far-off lands,
   And the blue sky bends over all.

"O bring back my lover once!" she cries,
   "As I sit by the sea alone;
O pitiful Father in Paradise!
   Stoop down from thy glorious throne,

O THE SEA, THE STORMY, TEMPESTUOUS SEA!

And grant to the light of my waiting eyes
One glimpse of his face,—only one!"

Now the sea rolls in with a mighty swell,—
Will it bring a curse or a crown?
For, alas! no echoing murmurs tell
Of the home-bound ship that went down
Mid the hidden reefs, with never a knell
From the slumbering harbor town.

All about her the water moans and raves,
She is drenched with the falling sleet;
Something lies dark in the arms of the waves
Where the sky and the waters meet:
Lo! a victim snatched from the coral graves
Is cast on the beach at her feet!

O beautiful Margaret, pale and fair!
By the sea no longer alone;
For two faces lie in the starlight there,
With features like chiselled stone.
And the seaweed drifts from his tangled hair
To the sunny locks of her own.

The Station Agent's Story.

TAKE a seat in the shade here, lady;
It 's tiresome, I know, to wait;
But when the train reaches Verona
It 's always sure to be late,—
'Specially when any one 's waitin'.
Been gatherin' flowers, I see?
Ah, well! they 're better company
Than a rough old fellow like me.

You noticed the graves 'neath the willows,
Down there where the blossoms grew?
Well, yes, there 's a story about them,
Almost too strange to be true;
'T is a stranger, sweeter story
Than was ever written in books;
And God made the endin' so perfect—
There, now I see by your looks

I will have to tell the story:
    Let me see; 't was eight years ago
One blusterin' night in winter,
    When the air was thick with snow;
As the freight came round the curve there
    They beheld a man on the track,
Bravin' the storm before him, but
    Not heedin' the foe at his back.

And ere a hand could grasp the bell-rope,
    Or a finger reach the rod,
One sweep from the cruel snow-plough
    Had sent the man's soul to its God!
They laid him out here in the freight-house,
    And I stayed with him that night;
He 'd one of the pleasantest faces,
    So hopeful and young and bright.

There was only a worn-out letter;
    I know it by heart — it said:
"Dear John: Baby May grows finely,
    I send you this curl from her head.
We will meet you at Brackenboro'.
    The grandfather 's sad and lone,

But I read him your kind words, sayin',
    When we 've a home of our own,

He shall sing the songs of old England
    Beneath our own willow tree."
That was all there was of it, lady,
    And 't was signed just "Alice Leigh."
So we made a grave in the mornin'
    And buried the man out there
Alone, unmourned, in a stranger's land,
    With only a stranger's prayer.

But when he 'd slept in his lonely grave
    Out there nigh on to a year,
Ray's freight ran into a washout
    By the culvert, away down here;
There were only two passengers that night,
    Dead when we found them there,—
A sweet little Englishwoman,
    And a baby with golden hair.

On her breast lay the laughing baby,
    With its rosy finger-tips

Still warm, and the fair young mother
With a frozen smile on her lips.
We laid them out here in the freight-house,
I stayed that night with the dead;
I shall never forget the letter
We found in her purse; it said:

"Dear Alice: Praise God I've got here!
I'll soon have a home for you now;
But you must come with the baby
As soon as you can anyhow.
Comfort the grandfather, and tell him
That by and by *he* shall come,
And sing the songs of old England
'Neath the willows beside our home;

For, close by the door of our cottage
I'll set out a willow tree,
For his sake and the sake of old England.
Lovingly yours. John Leigh."

The tears filled my eyes as I read it;
But I whispered, "God is just!"

For I knew the true heart yonder—
Then only a handful of dust—
Had drawn this sweet little woman
Right here, and God's merciful love
Had taken her from the sorrow
To the glad reunion above!

So, close by the grave of the other
We laid her away to rest,—
The golden-haired English mother,
With the baby upon her breast.
I planted those trees above them,
For I knew their story, you see;
And I thought their rest would be sweeter
'Neath their own loved willow tree.

Five years rolled along; and, lady,
My story may now seem to you
Like a wonderful piece of fiction;
But I tell you it is true,—
As true as that God is above us!
One summer day, hot and clear,

As the train rolled into the station
  And stopped to change engines here,

Among a company of Mormons
  Came a tremblin' white-haired man;
He asked me in waverin' accents,
  "Will you tell me, sir, if you can,
Of a place called Brackenboro'?
  And how far have I got to go?"
"It's the next station north," I answered,
  "Only thirteen miles below."

His old face lit up for a moment
  With a look of joy complete;
Then he threw up his hands toward Heaven,
  And dropped down dead at my feet!
"Old Hugh Leigh is dead!" said a Mormon,
  "And sights o' trouble he's be'n.
Nothin' would do when we started
  But that he must come with us then,

To find Alice, John, and the baby;
  And his heart was well-nigh broke

With waitin' and watchin' in England
For letters they never wrote."
So we buried him there with the others,
Beneath the willow tree.
'T was God's way of endin' the story —
More perfect than man's could be.

The Red Cross.

"YES, Louis, go! your country calls; I will not keep you here;
For every soldier in the field some heart holds just as dear,
And tears will come at parting which we vainly strive to hide;
Go! mid the busy din of war forget your English bride.

"But when the smoke has cleared away, and when the battle's done,
You'll think of her who prays for you from rise till set of sun,
And picture oft the brighter days, when, marching home with pride,
You'll gain a joyous welcome from your waiting English bride."

His firm hands clasped hers kindly, while his dark eyes searched her face,—
A face of woman's sweetness, with a gleam of tender grace;
But, oh! the woman's love was there, half worship and half pride,
As each fair feature quivered with the pain she could not hide.

"Give me one token, Bertha, of the love you bear for me,
That in my camp-life's duller hours will turn my thoughts to thee;
A ribbon you have worn will do: if these dear hands have pressed
Its silken folds, I'll wear it then forever on my breast."

She stood in thought one moment, then her fingers, white and fair
With gleaming scissors wandered in her mass of golden hair;
And as he held the token, that one little shining tress,
It twined around his finger with a loving, mute caress.

"This is the token, Louis, that will bid you think of me,
And may God's holy angels keep a watchful care o'er thee,—
To guide your steps in battle safe, unharmed from shot or shell;
But should you fall I'll try to say, '*He doeth all things well.*'"

"What! tears, my gentle Bertha? and I thought you were so brave!
We know the future, darling, holds many a soldier's grave,—
Holds many wives and orphans, who will wait and watch in vain
For the step and voice that never will greet their ear again."

Back from her pure white forehead he held the sunny hair,
And left a soldier's burning kiss of love and pity there,—

A soldier's tender, longing kiss — ah! many a heart can tell,
The saddest words in every tongue are those which say farewell.

Oh, weeks that drag their weary length along the shore of time!
Each night and morn the torture of suspense and fear combine
To rob the aching head of rest, to fill the heart with pain,
And with their slow, consuming fire at last to craze the brain.

Brave soldier in the field of strife, though hard your lot may be,
You cannot know the anxious hours she spends who waits for thee;
For wild imagination gives the sharpest pang we feel,
And each dread battle probes the wound with keener edge than steel.

O woman, toiling all the day mid hunger, want, and care,
With little space for thought or tears, and scarcely time for prayer!
Your labor is a blessing, for though deep your heartfelt pain,
You have no hours' maddening thoughts, and dreams that craze the brain.

There's always room for tender hands where wounded soldiers lie,
To bind the shattered broken limb, to close the sightless eye,
To pray before God's altar for many a hardened man,
And point the way to Heaven as only woman can.

When Bertha heard the summons as it came across the tide,
She laid all woman's weakness by, and, asking God to guide,
She left her northern home, with all its luxuries, to go
And join the "Red Cross" sisterhood mid scenes of pain and woe.

Many a dying soldier turned with wistful, longing eyes
To catch the blessed words she spoke of rest beyond the skies;
Some vaguely thought the girlish face, shaded by golden hair,
In their last hours was but a pure sweet angel bending there.

Oft to waiting wives and mothers she sent the message home,
In the place of many a loved one who nevermore would come,
And dropped a tear of pity for the homes made desolate,
Where now the golden dawn of peace would only come too late.

Once bending o'er a ghastly corpse, with scarred and mangled face,
She thought, could e'en his mother in those swollen features trace
One dear look to remind her of the son she sent away,
Unless she knew the wavy hair that round his temples lay?

What hushed her heart's wild throbbings then? what blanched her cheek so white?
"O God!" she cried, "it cannot be! but this dark hair is like —

EACH NIGHT AND MORN THE TORTURE OF SUSPENSE AND FEAR COMBINE
TO ROB THE ACHING HEAD OF REST, TO FILL THE HEART WITH PAIN.

So very much like Louis' hair, all bright and brown — but then
The battle-field is strewn with dead, and some are dark-haired men.

Just where a stinging death-winged ball had torn his coat apart,
And left a crimson, ragged rent above his loyal heart,
One little tress was clinging in the long, unseemly tear,
All matted in his heart's best gore, — a tress of golden hair.

With pallid cheek and dizzy brain she sank upon the floor:
'T is well that dark oblivion comes when hearts can bear no more.
But, oh! the wakening cometh too, with hopeless, maddening pain,
And memory points to happy hours that will not come again!

Back rushed the tide of life again to lip and cheek and brow;
'T was life without one ray of hope to cheer her future now;
'T was life — but oh! it seemed so long to toil and weep and wait!
For her the joyful morn of peace would dawn, but all too late!

Back to her work with softer light in her dark eyes she came;
Speaking sweet words of comfort with a healing balm, the same
As though her own heart suffered not, bravely she hid its pain,
And nursed health's bloom and courage back to faltering hearts again.

Just where the sun fell brightest on a weary boyish face,
A form convulsed with torture in the clasp of death's embrace,—
A white brow, fair and truthful, half concealed by nut-brown hair,—
Some loving mother's darling in his youth lay dying there.

And Bertha, kneeling by him, caught the accents of a prayer,
That he might die in his loved home, that vine-clad cottage where
His feet had roamed in brighter days; but ere the prayer was said
She closed the pleading, tearful eyes, for the boy's soul had fled.

The men who stood in waiting bore the slender form away,
While she smoothed the coarse, rough pillow where late his ringlets lay,
And sighed for those to whom the tale would carry untold pain,
As they laid another soldier where the dead boy's head had lain.

Pale, ghastly pale, his cheek and brow, and wild his wandering eye!
They told her that he could not live,—they 'd brought him there to die.
But in his face she saw a look that blanched her cheeks as white
As when she stood beside her dead, and every hope took flight.

O'er him her quivering face is bent; her cheeks now flushed, now white,
Her pale lips trembling and her eyes grown dark with hopeful light,

Within the soldier's blood-stained coat she lays her hand, and there
Her fingers clasp a shining curl,—"*Thank God! 't is golden hair!*"

'T was Louis! yes, and life was there, though flickering, faint, and dim.
Day after day with ceaseless care she watched and prayed for him;
And God, who hears these prayers of ours, and knows each sad heart's pain,
Into her faithful, loving hands gave back his life again.

Down the Track.

IN the deepening shades of twilight
  Stood a maiden, young and fair;
Rain-drops gleamed on cheek and forehead,
  Rain-drops glistened in her hair.
Where the bridge had stood at morning
  Yawned a chasm deep and black;
Faintly came the distant rumbling
  From the train far down the track.

Paler grew each marble feature;
  Faster came her frightened breath,—
Charlie kissed her lips at morning,—
  Charlie rushing down to death!
Must she stand and see him perish?
  Angry waters answer back;
Louder comes the distant rumbling
  From the train far down the track.

At death's door faint hearts grow fearless,
    Miracles are sometimes wrought,
Springing from the heart's devotion
    In the forming of a thought.
From her waist she tears her apron,
    Flings her tangled tresses back,
Working fast and praying ever
    For that train far down the track.

See! a lurid spark is kindled,
    Right and left she flings the flame,
Turns and speeds with airy fleetness
    Downward toward the coming train;
Sees afar the red eye gleaming
    Through the shadows dense and black.
Hark! a shriek prolonged and deafening,—
    They have seen her down the track!

Onward comes the train,—now slower,
    But the maiden, where is she?
Flaming torch and flying footsteps,
    Fond eyes gaze in vain to see.
With a white face turned to heaven,
    All her sunny hair thrown back,

There they found her, one hand lying
Crushed and bleeding on the track.

Eager faces bent above her,
Wet eyes pitied, kind lips blest;
But she saw no face save Charlie's,—
'T was for him she saved the rest.
Gold they gave her from their bounty;
But her sweet eyes wandered back
To the face whose love will scatter
Roses all along life's track.

In the Mining Town.

"'Tis the last time, darling," he gently said,
As he kissed her lips like the cherries red,
While a fond look shone in his eyes of brown:
"My own is the prettiest girl in town.
To-morrow the bell from the tower will ring
A joyful peal. Was there ever a king
So truly blest, on his royal throne,
As I shall be when I claim my own!"

'Twas a fond farewell; 'twas a sweet good-by;
But she watched him go with a troubled sigh,
As into the basket, that swayed and swung
O'er the yawning abyss, he lightly sprung;
And the joy of her heart seemed turned to woe
As they lowered him into the depths below.
Her sweet young face, with its tresses brown,
Was the fairest face in the mining town.

Lo the morning came! but the marriage-bell
High up in the tower rang a mournful knell
For the true heart buried 'neath earth and stone,
Far down in the heart of the mine alone,—
A sorrowful peal on their wedding-day
For the breaking heart and the heart of clay;
And the face that looked from her tresses brown
Was the saddest face in the mining town.

Thus time rolled along on its weary way,
Until fifty years with their shadows gray
Had darkened the light of her sweet eyes' glow,
And had turned the brown of her hair to snow.
Oh! never a kiss from a husband's lips,
Or the clasp of a child's sweet finger-tips,
Had lifted one moment the shadows brown
From the saddest heart in the mining town!

Far down in the depths of the mine, one day
In the loosened earth they were digging away,
They discovered a face, so young, so fair;
From the smiling lip to the bright brown hair
Untouched by the finger of Time's decay.
When they drew him up to the light of day

The wondering people gathered round
To gaze at the man thus strangely found.

Then a woman came from among the crowd,
With her long white hair, and her slight form bowed.
She silently knelt by the form of clay,
And kissed the lips that were cold and gray.
Then the sad old face, with its snowy hair
On his youthful bosom lay pillowed there.
He had found her at last his waiting bride,
And the people buried them side by side.

In Answer.

"MADAM, we miss the train at B——."
"But can't you make it, sir?" she gasped.
"Impossible! it leaves at three,
And we are due a quarter past."
"Is there no way? Oh! tell me, then,
Are you a Christian?" "I am not."
"And are there none among the men
Who run the train?" "No — I forgot —
I think this fellow over here,
Oiling the engine, claims to be."
She turned upon the engineer
A fair face white with agony.

"Are you a Christian?" "Yes, I am."
"Then, O, sir! won't you pray with me,

All the long way, that God will stay,
That God will hold the train at B——?"
"'Twill do no good. It leaves at three,
And—" "Yes, but God *can* hold the train;
My dying child is calling me,
And I *must* see her face again.
Oh! *won't you* pray?" "I will!" a nod
Emphatic, as he takes his place.
When Christians grasp the arm of God
They grasp the power that rules the race.

Out from the station swept the train
On time,—swept on past wood and lea;
The engineer, with cheeks aflame,
Prayed, "O Lord, hold the train at B——!"
Then flung the throttle wide, and like
Some giant monster of the plain,
With panting sides and mighty strides,
Past hill and valley swept the train.

A half,—a minute,—two are gained;
Along those burnished lines of steel
His glances leap, each nerve is strained,
And still he prays with fervent zeal.

Heart, hand, and brain with one accord
  Work while his prayer ascends to Heaven:
"Just hold the train eight minutes, Lord,
  And I'll make up the other seven."

With rush and roar through meadow lands,
  Past cottage homes and green hillsides,
The panting thing obeys his hands,
  And speeds along with giant strides.
They say an accident delayed
  The train a little while; but He
Who listened while His children prayed,
  In answer held the train at B——.

THE BRIDGE OF SAN MARTIN.

"GO build the bridge o' San Martin across the rapid stream;
Across the dashing Tagus, whose waters flash and gleam,
Whose angry, raging billows, foam-crested as they flow,
Send back a roar defiant from out the depths below."

"But who shall plan the structure?" Black sweeps the swollen tide,
While anxious faces gather dark-browed on either side.
And, lo! before Tenorio a youthful form appears,
Tall, dark, and slender, seeming a very boy in years.

"But what pledge can *you* offer, that our trust be not vain?"
Across the young face hopeful there swept a dash of pain.
A glance, half love, half pity, he gave his girlish wife,
Then said: "I pledge my honor,—my honor and my life.

"When they remove the scaffold which holds the arch of stone,
I'll stand upon the centre of the great new bridge alone.
And if the crowning glory of all my heart's desire
Is wrecked, with it I perish. What more would you require?"

Behold the work completed! To-morrow's light shall see
The great bridge of San Martin from all support cut free!
But he who watched its progress with heart and eye aglow
Beside fair Catalina sits wrapt in deepest woe.

"To-morrow morn the people will gather on the shore,
And I shall see the sun rise o'er Spain's green hills once more;
Once more I'll clasp you, darling, close to my breaking heart,
Before that awful moment in which I take a part.

"A single fatal error! To-morrow's sun will gleam
Upon the bridge and builder wrecked on the raging stream.
Ah! death indeed were welcome, forgetfulness were kind,
To veil the dark dishonor and shame I leave behind."

No word spoke Catalina, but when he sought his bed
To the bridge of San Martin she flew with noiseless tread.

THE BRIDGE OF SAN MARTIN.

A lurid spark she kindled, the night-winds fanned the flame,
And soon the fiery billows had saved her husband's name.

The new bridge of San Martin from out the dust and flame
Reared high in massive grandeur, a monument of fame
To crown the youthful builder. Complete in every part,
His name 's enshrined with honor in every Spaniard's heart.

THANKSGIVING DAY.

THE floor had been swept, and the furniture dusted,
The table white spread in the neat dining-hall;
The cakes on the pantry shelf, pure snowy crusted,
And pies, custard, pumpkin, mince, apple, and all,
With pans full of doughnuts and cookies, were waiting
To fill up the table in splendid array;
The chickens and turkeys were quietly baking,
And all things were ready for Thanksgiving day.

Once again Grandma Snow looked in at the baking,
While Grandpa looked anxiously out at the door,
Some sweet, tender thought in their bosoms awaking
Of life's holy mission so soon to be o'er.
At last all was done. By the fire brightly burning
They sat, those two loving ones, aged and gray,
And talked of the children now gladly returning
To father and mother this Thanksgiving day.

"It's time they were comin'; why, do you know, mother,
 It seems but a day since the children were here?
A bright, noisy group, playing tag with each other,
 And now they come home to us just once a year.
Little Mary will come, our dear little Mary —
 Who'd think of our baby as going away
With a stranger! and Tom, from the distant prairie.
 Ah, well! they'll be with us this Thanksgiving day.

"And Dick, from down South, with his fine, pretty lady, —
 I hope she won't scorn us, and our humble home."
"And Florence," said Grandma, "will come with her baby,
 And Susan, with all the dear children, will come.
Well, well! they will find us here ready to meet them, —
 We keep the nest warm when our birds are away, —
And in the dear home of their childhood we'll greet them
 At least once a year, on the Thanksgiving day.

"The years seem so bright since you brought me here, Peter;
 Your love made them peaceful and happy and long."
"And, Mary," said he, "you are dearer and sweeter
 Than ever you were in the years that are gone.
We've come down the hill of life's journey together,
 Through sunshine and shade, side by side all the way;

Your lover, who told you his love by the river,
Is your true lover still, on this Thanksgiving day.

"When our last one left us, dear heart, how we missed her!
But now they 're all settled in homes of their own.
Our life work is finished," — he bent over and kissed her, —
"In the empty home nest we are waiting alone."
With his arm round her waist, her head on his shoulder,
His hand clasping hers in the old loving way,
They 're roaming, once more, by the stream where he told her
His love long ago on a Thanksgiving day.

He is telling it over, the sweet, olden story!
Forgetting the years and the sorrows between;
The sunlight creeps in with a halo of glory, —
Creeps in through the window, unheeded, unseen.
There 's a rumbling of wheels, and glad, happy voices;
Men, women, and children, in festive array,
Come down the long walk — how each fond heart rejoices
In this glad reunion on Thanksgiving day!

His hand clasping hers, the aged couple are sitting,
The room has grown chill, for the fire has gone out;

The kitten is playing with grandmother's knitting,—
They heed not the children who gather about.
They heed not, they care not, for over the river
The dusky-winged angel hath borne them away!
Hand in hand, side by side, crossed over together,
Life crowned with eternity's Thanksgiving day.

The Soldier's Reprieve.

"MY Fred! I can't understand it,"
  And his voice quivered with pain,
While the tears kept slowly dropping
  On his trembling hands like rain.
"For Fred was so brave and loyal,
  So true — but my eyes are dim,
And I cannot read the letter,
  The last I shall get from him.
Please read it, sir, while I listen —
  In fancy I see him — dead;
My boy, shot down like a traitor,
  My noble, my brave boy Fred."

"Dear Father," — so ran the letter, —
  "To-morrow when twilight creeps
Along the hill to the churchyard,
  O'er the grave where mother sleeps,
When the dusky shadows gather,
  They 'll lay your boy in his grave

For nearly betraying the country
He would give his life to save.
And, father, I tell you truly,
With almost my latest breath,
That your boy is not a traitor,
Though he dies a traitor's death.

"You remember Bennie Wilson?
He's suffered a deal of pain.
He was only *that* day ordered
Back into the ranks again.
I carried all of his luggage,
With mine, on the march that day;
I gave him my arm to lean on,
Else he had dropped by the way.
'T was Bennie's turn to be sentry;
But I took his place, and I —
Father, I fell asleep, and now
I must die as traitors die.

"The Colonel is kind and generous,
He has done the best he can,
And they will not bind or blind me —
I shall meet death like a man.

Kiss little Blossom; but, father,
Need you tell her how I fall?"
A sob from the shadowed corner,—
Yes, Blossom had heard it all!
As she kissed the precious letter
She said with faltering breath,
"Our Fred is never a traitor,
Though he dies a traitor's death."

And a little sun-brown maiden,
In a shabby time-worn dress,
Took her seat a half-hour later
In the crowded night express.
The conductor heard her story
As he held her dimpled hand,
And sighed for the sad hearts breaking
All over the troubled land.
He tenderly wiped the teardrop
From the blue eyes brimming o'er,
And guarded her footsteps safely
Till she reached the White House door.

The President sat at his writing;
But the eyes were kind and mild

That turned with a look of wonder
    On the little shy-faced child.
And he read Fred's farewell letter
    With a look of sad regret.
"'T is a brave young life," he murmured,
    "And his country needs him yet.
From an honored place in battle
    He shall bid the world good-by;
If that brave young life is needed,
    He shall die as heroes die."

The Luck of Muncaster.

A LEGEND OF MERRIE ENGLAND.

BESIDE the crystal well she stood,
Fair Margaret, Lowther's daughter,
Clear hazel eyes smiled back at her
Up from the sparkling water.
The sunlight fell on tresses bright,
Tresses half brown, half golden,
While at her feet Lord William knelt,
And told the story olden.

An outlaw border chieftain he,
Of haughty mien and carriage,
With earnest words on bended knee
Besought her hand in marriage.
"My life with thine," the lady said,
"Can never be united;
To brave Sir John of Muncaster
This hand of mine is plighted."

"My vengeance," cried the dark-browed Scot,
"On thee, proud Lowther's daughter!
This lord of thine shall not be safe
From me on land or water!"
Disdainful smiled the lady then:
"Thy threats are unavailing;
While Sir John owns the sacred cup,
Mischance can ne'er assail him.

"'Twas Henry Sixth pronounced the charm
(A glass cup was the token),
'In Muncaster good luck shall reign
Till this charmed cup is broken!'
A hundred years the charm hath held
Its power beyond undoing;
Good luck attends Muncaster lords
In battle and in wooing."

"And this the luck of Muncaster?"
Said the rejected lover.
"The charm hath stood a hundred years,
It shall not stand another."
Then straight to Carlisle tower he rode:
"My lord," he cried, "make ready,

For Douglas comes with Scottish hordes!
Each arm is strong and steady.

"Prepare to give them battle now,
And mete out justice measure;
Or send some trusted messenger
For thy most valued treasure."
"Small treasure have I," Sir John said,
"But one in casket oaken
I fain would save from plundering hand,
Untarnished and unbroken.

"Go thou and bring the gem I prize;
Thou art no foe or stranger,
Else why hast rode this weary way
To warn me of my danger?"
And ere the bat had winged its flight
Across night's sable curtain
The dark-browed knight of Liddersdale
Had done the message certain.

"Now, by my lady's lips, I swear,
Thy friendship is amazing,"

TWO THOUSAND SOLDIERS CAME IN TIME
TO STAY THE DOUGLAS SLAUGHTER,
AND GAY SIR JOHN WAS MARRIED TO
FAIR MARGARET, LOWTHER'S DAUGHTER.

Cried gay Sir John of Muncaster,
Into the dark face gazing.
"Swear not by lips of her you love, —
You never more shall press them;
Bright are the locks of Margaret's hair, —
No more shalt thou caress them."

Exclaimed the fiery Scot in glee,
"I hold the precious token
That binds good luck to thee and thine, —
That charmed spell shall be broken.
Behold I dash it to the earth!
In vain thy deepest regret;
Douglas shall win thy palace tower,
And *I* the lady Marg'ret."

The traitor fled; Sir John sank down
Beside the casket oaken:
O miracle! the crystal cup
Lay there unharmed, unbroken!
Two thousand soldiers came in time
To stay the Douglas slaughter,
And gay Sir John was married to
Fair Margaret, Lowther's daughter.

The Little Bells.

A LEGEND OF THE FUCHSIA.

CLASPING her close in his strong young arms,
  As his blue eyes met her own,
He said: "I have brought a lovely plant
  From the far-off tropic zone,
With clusters of leaves like satin green,
  And blossoms — ah, who can tell? —
Some day you will see each bud will be
  A wonderful little bell.

"Though sorrow comes to your waiting heart
  When my ship has sailed away,
Remember I said, 'These bells will ring
  On your happy wedding-day.'
A fortune I've brought you, sister mine,
  From the sun-crowned southern dells;
Go and set it where the sweet south air
  Will open the little bells."

In the southern window, bright and warm,
'Neath the low-roofed cottage eaves,
She placed her treasure, and day by day
She watched its unfolding leaves;
There were tears in her sweet English eyes,
Tears gleamed on her lashes brown,
For a ship one day, far, far away
In a storm-tossed sea went down.

The young earl rode by the cot one day
When the plant was all in bloom;
He lingered long ere he rode away
In the dusk of twilight's gloom.
"The loveliest flowers on earth," he said,
"They bloom by a cottage wall;
They would grace a throne; they shall be my own,
And bloom in my palace hall."

He met the maid at the cottage door:
"A fortune," he said, "for these."
"No, no," she cried, as a vision came
Of the stormy southern seas,
"The hand that gave them lies cold and still
In one of the ocean dells;

It would break my heart to ever part
With my dainty little bells."

He turned his gaze on the maiden's face, —
A face that was shy and sweet;
She was wondrous fair, from her gold-kissed hair
To her pretty sandalled feet.
"'T is the fairest face on earth," he thought,
"As pure as an angel's own;
She shall be my bride; 't is a shame to hide
Such grace in a cottage home!"

O, the palace halls were wide and grand,
And the palace towers were high!
There were lawns and parks wide spreading 'neath
The dome of the English sky.
And still to the listening children
At twilight a grandsire tells
Of a lady bright who was wed one night
Mid the chime of little bells.

"THE LOVELIEST FLOWERS ON EARTH," HE SAID.
"THEY BLOOM BY A COTTAGE WALL."

Drinking Annie's Tears.

"MY treat, boys? Step up! I don't care if I do!
It's many a time I've been treated by you;
And, boys, I can tell you, it's many a timo
With you at the bar I have spent my last dime,
And gone reeling home; but you've both done the same;
We began, I believe, with wine and champagne
Served in wafer-like glasses, thin as the mist
That rolls from the sea which the sun-god has kissed.

"We were then college students; science and rhyme,
Art, music, and Latin, slipped down with our wine;
But stomach and brain got o'er-loaded, and so
We held to the drinks and let all the rest go.
Success we had painted in glow-light of pride,—
Ambition and wealth swept away by the tide,—
Love, social position, and friends by the score,—
We sacrificed all, but the demon craves more!
We gave him each one of life's blessings, 't is true:
He asks for our souls, and eternity too!

"Step up, boys! it's my treat,—providing you'll take
The beverage I've chosen for old friendship's sake.

"You wonder what mixture I've gotten up now?
No mixed drink for me! I am sure you'll allow
I have mixed my drinks well,—rum, beer, and champagne:
Strong drink in the stomach is death to the brain,
And death to affection. Deny it, who can?
A drunkard has only the semblance of man,
The form of his Maker, degraded, accursed,
The vilest of all living things, and the worst.

"But sometimes that bit of God's presence within,
Which clings to a fellow in spite of his sin,
And sets him to thinking,—well, sometimes you know
The angel within us has worried us so
We have sworn to reform. We did it last year,
When we pledged to drink nothing stronger than beer.

"We made up in quantity what lacked in fire,
And watched the last glow of true manhood expire
In excuses, poor phantoms! pride's tawdry hearse
Concealing—not death—but humanity's curse.

We satisfied conscience, hushed whisperings of fear,
We three model temperance men drinking our beer.

"Drinks for three, if you please. We'll take the pure stuff!
Of soul-blighting mixtures we've had quite enough.
Don't scrimp the measure! fill the glass to the brim,
With God's sparkling sunlight and glory thrown in.
Pure crystallized light from the vineyards above,
Drink fit for the gods from God's wine-press of love!

"What brought it about, this free lecture of mine?
What stirred up the depths of my soul against wine,
And wine's variations? List, boys, while I tell:
You know how you left me that night at the well,
Blear-eyed and besotted, with imbecile leer,—
A real model temperance man pickled in beer!

"*She* met me, my guardian angel, so fair;
The night dews lay damp on her beautiful hair,
The heart dews hung wet on her lashes, and lay
On her thin, pallid cheeks. Boys, you know the day
She came to my home, wife and helpmeet to be,—
The bonniest girl, and you both envied me.

"The bright pansy blue has gone out of her eyes,
And her roses — oh! how I loathe and despise
The wretch who could blight them! No word of complaint
Or censure for me had my fair little saint.
She steadied my uncertain footsteps, and led
The wreck of my manhood, in silence, to bed.

"I called for a drink as the demon of thirst —
The demon whose presence my life has accursed —
Raged within me. Annie obeyed my command,
And brought me a drink with love's unweary hand.

"As she passed it to me one jewelled tear fell
And was lost in the water she brought from the well.
That tear sobered me. I had seen them before,
But I swore then and there I'd drink them no more.
I vowed that the rest of my life's unspent years
I'd drink God's pure water, but not Annie's tears."

A BRAVE EMPEROR.

NIGHT rolled its sombre curtain back
    To greet the dawning day,
Black swept the angry Danube
    On its terror-freighted way.
Great blocks of ice came crashing down
    Amid the torrent's roar,
And seething waters flung their spray
    Upon the ice-bound shore.

Across that raging, roaring space
    Where Leopoldstadt lies,
Back to Vienna's listening ear
    Came moans and sobs and cries,—
Came piteous voices pleading,
    "We are starving! bring us bread!"
And white hands reached imploring
    O'er the waters dark and dread.

The Emperor Francis Second
    Soon filled the boats with food;

But who will face the dangers
  Of this angry, seething flood?
He begs, implores, and threatens:
  Bribes and promises are vain,
While from his famished people
  Comes that anguished wail again.

"I cannot see my people starve!"
  The Emperor Francis cries;
A quiver thrills his earnest voice,
  A moisture dims his eyes.
Alone he leaps into a boat
  And pushes from the shore;
"They 'd give their lives for me," he said,
  "And I can do no more."

A hundred men are ready now
  To brave the swollen tide.
If death must come to their brave king,
  They 'll meet it at his side.
Behold they reach the distant shore!
  The hungry ones are fed;
And mothers kiss the hands that bring
  Their starving children bread!

"WE ARE STARVING! BRING US BREAD!"

THE QUEEN AND THE BEGGAR'S CHILD.

SILK and diamonds and trailing lace,
Haughty carriage and fair proud face;
Out from the palace towering high
Grand and gray 'neath the bending sky,
O'er the lawn with its carpet green,
Lightly stepping, came Austria's Queen,
Flashing gems in the summer's sun,
Tender Mother and Queen in one.

Jewels gleam on her royal hands,
Clasp her arms with their shining bands,
Sparkle and glow where the sunbeams fall;
But the most precious of them all
The nurse is holding with tender care,—
The royal baby, rosy and fair;
Pressing fond kisses on cheek and brow,
The Queen is only a Mother now.

Down the lawn, in its shadow deep,
A beggar-woman lies asleep.
Hunger, poverty, pain, and care
Darken the face once young and fair;
There by the wayside, seeking rest,
Clasping a babe upon her breast,
Its hungry wail across the green
Stirs the heart of the Mother Queen.

Down on the green grass kneeling low,
Baring her bosom as white as snow,
Laying the child without a name
Where only royal babes have lain,
Feeding it from her own proud breast.
Hungry, starving,—ah! there's the test,—
Mother-love spans the chasm wide;
Queen and station must stand aside!

Love's Avowal.

Dear heart of my heart,
Throbbing close to my breast
With fondest and truest pulsation,
List while I repeat
The old story, my sweet,
In the language of love's adoration!
O, life of my life,
All the purest and best
Of my manhood warms in thy presence,
No unworthy part
Of my life or my heart
Has a share in the sweet of love's essence.

Pure soul of my soul,
Is there aught in my past
I would blush for your eyes to discover?
You have reared my throne,
With your fair hands, my own,

You have crowned me your king, your true lover.
O, pure heart and true,
All my future for you
Shall read clear as the spring's crystal water,
Thou lily-white dove,
In the arms of my love
I will shield you, my fair little daughter!

Lost at Sea.

I STOOD where the starlit heavens
  Spread away over field and glen,
Like the hands of loving angels
  Reaching down to the hearts of men.

And the sea, with a glow, reflected
  The infinite lights above;
The quivering resplendent heavens
  All smiling with peaceful love.

And the waves o'er the white sand creeping
  Brought ripples of joyous glee,
As the lips of the purple heaven
  Bent over to kiss the sea.

"O treacherous sea!" I murmured,
  "Restore to my arms, I pray,
The treasure I gave to your keeping
  One beautiful autumn day."

A ship with its precious burden
Sailed out from my longing gaze,
Away from the peaceful harbor
In the bright October haze.

And a sweet face looking backward,
With a tear and a smile for me,—
The dearest of all my treasures
I gave to the treacherous sea.

Old Ocean, all darkly hidden
In thy secret bosom lies
The face that I fondly cherished,
The beautiful lovelit eyes.

For the ship that left the harbor
In the calm October haze
Bore its precious freight forever
Away from my longing gaze.

Kisses.

LITTLE child, when twilight shadows
   Close the western gates of gold,
Then those loving arms of mother's
   Tenderly about thee fold.
Over lip and cheek and forehead
   Like a shower caresses fall;
For a mother's kiss at twilight
   Is the sweetest kiss of all.

Slender maiden, at the gateway,
   Shy, sweet face and downcast eyes,
Two fair trembling hands imprisoned,
   Swift each golden moment flies;
Lips that softly press thy forehead
   All the rosy blushes call;
For a lover's kiss at evening
   Is the fondest kiss of all.

Happy wife, thy noble husband,
  More than half a lover yet,
For those sunny hours of wooing
  Are too sweet to soon forget;
On thy smiling mouth uplifted
  Tenderly his kisses fall;
For a husband's kiss at parting
  Is the dearest kiss of all.

Weary mother, little children
  With their dimpled hands so fair,
O'er thy tired face passing lightly,
  Soothe away the pain and care,
Lead your troubled thoughts to Heaven
  Where no dreary shadows fall;
For the kiss of little children
  Is the purest kiss of all.

OVER LIP AND CHEEK AND FOREHEAD LIKE A SHOWER, CARESSES FALL.

Two Pictures.

SUNSET.

A BALL of fire suspended
Low o'er a molten sea;
Infinite glory blended,
Lost in eternity.
A vivid crimson paling
With pencilings of gold;
A white cloud outward sailing,
Foam billows fold on fold.
A quivering, throbbing rapture,
Red torches flaming high;
A thousand waves that capture
Pale rose-tints from the sky;
A lesser glory, blending
With blue more faintly blue,
A rosy light ascending
To pierce all distance through.

Commingling tints grown fainter,
  A "dim fire," burning low,—
Ah, never skill of painter
  Can mix the colors so!
A mellowed beauty lingers,
  A curtain pearly gray
Is drawn by unseen fingers
  Across the face of Day.

Gone the resplendent wonder,—
  God's glory passed away,
We stand the gray sky under
  Beside a sea of gray,
And sigh because life's story,
  Like sunset's fleeting kiss,
Tells tales of transient glory,
  Lost rapture, vanished bliss.

SUNRISE.

SILENCE profound, then faintly
  Low throbbings in the air;
A presence holy, saintly,
  Hushed voices breathing prayer,

A wavering light uncertain,
  A soft glow, spreading wide;
A dusky, sombre curtain
  Drawn suddenly aside;
Pale rays of rare completeness
  Far down the sky's dim lawn,
Moist lips of rosy sweetness
  Upraised to kiss the dawn;
A wondrous burst of rapture
  From bird-throats swelling long,
Which echo elves recapture
  And flood the earth with song.

A richer color showing,
  A flush across the gray,
A deeper carmine glowing,
  Night shadows rolled away;
A gleam of polished silver,
  A glow of burnished gold,
A liquid mass of splendor,
  A glory manifold;
A royal car suspended,
  Hung swaying in the blue,
The grand cor'nation 's ended
  And rose-tints fade from view.

O, human heart grown tender
With thought beyond all speech!
This sunrise scene of splendor
No human art can reach
Revives hope's blessed story,
Bids faith ascend on high,
And view eternal glory
Where rose-tints never die.

How the Flowers Came.

'TWAS seed-time in Heaven; the angel whose care
Is for Eden's blossoms, — that angel more fair
Than all her fair sisters, twin spirits of air, —
That angel whose footsteps, wherever they tread,
Spring up into blossoms blue, yellow, and red, —
That angel whose tear-drops, wherever they fall,
Give birth to white lilies, the fairest of all, —
That angel whose breath is the perfume of flowers,
Had spent all the jewel-gemmed paradise hours
Of the roseate morn where beauties unfold
In calyx of crimson and purple and gold.

Beside the great portals she paused and looked through,
Down, down the vast distance of star-lighted blue, —
Beheld the gray rocks without beauty or bloom,
And sighed for earth's children away in the gloom.

"No beauty or bloom have the children of woe;
No brightness, no sweetness; my hand will bestow
One heaven-born seed for their garden below,"

She said as she loosened her girdle to find
One seed which was fairest, and best of its kind.
Her eager hand trembled, the girdle slipped through
Her rosy-tipped fingers, and down through the blue,
Down, down the vast distance, her golden seeds flew.

Some caught in the crevice of rocks, others fell
In lone desert places, by wayside and dell;
On hills and in valleys, in forest and glen,
To gladden and brighten the journeys of men

At the portals of heaven, with sorrowful face,
The little flower-angel looks out into space
In search of her treasures. Her tears, as they fall,
Find all her lost seedlings, and water them all.

Remember the Alamo!

THE WAR-CRY AT SAN JACINTO, TEXAS.

TWO student lads one morning met
Under the blue-domed Texas skies;
Strangers by birth and station, yet
Youth's heart lies close beneath youth's eyes.
A thousand miles lay 'twixt their homes,
Watered by many a crystal stream;
Dame Nature reared a thousand domes,
And spread a thousand plains between.
They met, clasped hands, scorned bolt and bar,
Which cautious age puts on the heart;
Shared room and purse, then wandered far
By quiet ways and busy mart.
By San Antonio's winding stream,
Through narrow streets, the two lads passed,
Saw antique ruins, like some dream
Of ancient times.

They came, at last,
Where the Alamo's moss-grown walls
Stand gray and silent in the sun.
Where'er its sombre shadow falls
Is hallowed ground,—more sacred none!

Within its portals stood a man
Like some grim shadow on Time's shore,
Gray as the walls about him, and
Like them a memory, nothing more,—
A page from out the deathless past!
Through film of years and rising smoke
From his old pipe he saw at last
The stranger lads, then gravely spoke:

"Come you to worship at our shrine,
The shrine o' Texas liberty?
Or come to speed the work o' time,
An' mar these stones grown dear to me?
Rome had her heroes, so have we;
I don't know what the big word means,
But this is *our* Thermopylæ,
An' matches Rome's for bloody scenes.
My story?

'COME YOU TO WORSHIP AT OUR SHRINE,
THE SHRINE O' TEXAS' LIBERTY?"

"'T is n't much to tell,
'T was more to live, but e'en that seems
At times a sort o' misty spell,—
A somethin' shaped from dreamin' dreams.
An' then again 't is wondrous real;
I seem to see the smokin' plains,
I hear the cannon's roar, an' feel
The young blood rushin' through my veins;
For I was with Sam Houston there
At San Jacinto. All the tricks
That sneakin' Mexicans will dare,
An' did, we paid in '36.

"We were three brothers. Brother Jim
The tallest, stoutest o' the three,
Then me, hot-headed, next to him,
An' Will was mother's pet, you see!
For Will was slender, like a girl,
Brave to the heart an' true as steel;
An' me an' Jim, 'long side o' him,
Were not much 'count.

"The past seems real
Enough just now. My eyes are dim,
Grown weak with years. Well, lads, we three

Shouldered our muskets. Brother Jim
 Was here with Travis. Will an' me
Heard how our Texas heroes fought
 With death behind an' death before,
To right an' left o' them, an' naught
 But death when they could fight no more.
It fires my blood to think o' it,
 The desperate scene comes back to me,
How, like wild beasts trapped in a pit
 They fought, as round 'em surged a sea
O' swarthy faces, black with hate
 Like their black hearts.

"Six thousand strong
They swarmed about, nor wall nor gate
 Nor rifle-shot could hold 'em long.
Like flies about a pot o' sweet,
 Like savage fiends let loose from hell,
Like starvin' wolves in sight o' meat,
 They filled the place.

"There Crockett fell,
 Here Bowie, on his dyin' bed
Was butchered, so was all o' them.

This room was filled with Texans dead,
    The bravest, truest, *best* o' men."

The old man paused. Low drooped his head;
    Upon his breast his beard lay white.
"These dead men nerved our arms," he said,
    "For somethin' more than human might.
Will flushed up when he spoke Jim's name;
    There was n't time for weepin' then,
But in his eyes I saw the flame
    That burns the softness out o' men.

"We were at Colita. Mayhap you
    Have read the story? Fannin's men
'Gainst fearful odds surrendered. True
    Their numbers sort o' scart us then,
But later we forgot all fear,
    An' fought like men gone sudden mad.
They wrote their own death-warrant *here,*
    But *it was signed at Goliad.*
Yes, we were prisoners, confined
    At Goliad, but soon to be
Sent home, an' so we did n't mind
    Our prison-walls, for Will an' me
Still had each other.

"That last night
We, a right jolly set o' men,
Sang 'Home, sweet Home,' with all our might,
An' talked o' home like boys o' ten.
I reckon that with home so near
An' mother, too, we grew a bit
Soft-hearted. Will dashed off a tear
Quick like as if ashamed o' it,
An' me —

"Well, mornin' came, an' we
Was ordered out. The air was sweet
With scent o' flowers. I seem to see
The posies noddin' at our feet,
As their wee faces nodded there
Beside the Mission walls, where we
In long lines stood with freezin' blood
A-waitin' for the liberty
They promised us. My God! it came
Too soon! 'T was home we'd thought about,
An' wife an' child, but not the flame
O' death that let our life-blood out.
One wild thought o' the future, then
A flash o' fire an' nothin'ness.
Shot down like dogs. Three hundred men
Sent home! 'T was murder, nothin' less.

"All day I lay still feignin' death
Among the dead, an' when the night
Came down, I searched with pantin' breath
For Will's dead face, in the dim light.
Yes, lads, I found him where he fell,
An', kneelin' 'neath the starry skies—
Mayhap 't want soldier-like, but—well
I choked, an' somethin' filled my eyes.

"I can't tell how I got away.
I reckon angel wings swooped down,
An' sort o' hid me night an' day,
For eyes were peerin' all around.
An' *I* was saved. I don't know why,
Unless God sent an' drafted me
From 'mong the dead to start the cry
That gave us Texas liberty.
How did it end?

"No Texas lad
Would ask me that. I reckon you
Came from the North? Well, lads, we had
Our 'counts all ready, what was due
Us marked in figures plain, then we

At San Jacinto took our pay,
The price we set was *Liberty;*
An' it was paid that very day,
An' they were two to one of us;
But we went in for vengeance then.
The Alamo dead stood side of us,
An' gave each man the strength o' ten.
The plan o' battle?

"I can't tell,
My brain, somehow, forgets the plan,
But white flowers turned to red where fell
Each sneakin', savage Mexican.
The debt o' blood we paid in blood:
'*Remember, boys, the Alamo!*'
Fired every Texan where he stood,
An' nerved his arm for deadly blow.
We whipped 'em, lads, an' Liberty
Was born, that day, through fire an' smoke.
This one old comrade 's left to me."
He lit his clay pipe as he spoke.

Historical Notes.

"Remember the Alamo!" tells its own story; and to those who have lived within the shadow of the Alamo's historic walls the poem will be sufficient for itself, but to those whose hearts have never thrilled with the story of Texas blood-bought freedom, to whom its history is not familiar, these explanatory notes, together with a few historic facts, gleaned from "Thrall's History of Texas," will be necessary for the more perfect understanding of those "truths which are stranger than fiction."

The Alamo is appropriately called the "Thermopylæ of Texas." Here Travis and his heroic band re-enacted the part performed by the brave Spartans nearly twenty-three centuries before.

Santa Anna having gained a decisive victory over Governor Garcia, to the total destruction of the republican party in Mexico, began preparations for the subjugation of Texas.

On the 22d of February, 1836, a portion of the invading army reached the Alazan creek, a little west of the city of San Antonio, when Colonel Travis, with one hundred and forty-five effective men, retired to the fortress of the Alamo.

February 23, about noon Santa Anna arrived in person, and sent a summons to the Texans to surrender. It was answered by a cannon-shot. In Travis's despatch, sent by a courier to Goliad, he said: "I shall never surrender or retreat."

For ten days the siege continued with unabated fury. On the tenth day Travis sent out a courier with this message: "I have held this place for ten days against a force variously estimated at from 1500 to 6000, and I shall continue to hold it till I get relief from my countrymen, or I will perish in its defence."

Travis now despaired of succor, and after declaring his determination to sell his life as dearly as possible, and drawing a line with his sword, Travis exhorted all who were willing to fight with him to the last to form on the line. With one exception all fell into the ranks, and even Bowie, who was dying with consumption, had his cot carried to the line.

Sunday, March 6th, witnessed the fall of the Alamo, and the brutal slaughter of its brave defenders, for the feeble garrison could no longer hold out against such overwhelming numbers. Travis fell early in the action, shot with a rifle-ball in the head. The body of Crockett was in the yard, with a number of Mexicans lying near him. Bowie was slain in his bed. The sacrifice was complete; every soldier had fallen in defence of the fort.

The battle of Colita, with Colonel Fannin commanding the Texas army, resulted in their surrender. With no adequate protection against the enemy's cannon, in an open prairie, without water, surrounded by an enemy of five times their number, the Texans were in a desperate condition. They surrendered as prisoners of war, with the agreement that they were to be sent to Copano, and thence, in eight days, to the United States, or as soon as vessels could be procured to take them.

The prisoners were taken back to Goliad and confined in the old Mission. All were cheerful in the prospect of a speedy liberation. While they were enlivening their prison, on the evening of the 26th of March, in singing 'Home, Sweet Home,' an order arrived from Santa Anna for their immediate execution!

On the morning of the 27th, Palm Sunday, without warning, and under the pretext that they were starting for home, they were marched out, and when a short distance from the walls of the Mission were halted and shot! The most were instantly killed, some who were only wounded were despatched with sabres, and a few, by lying still and feigning death until dark, escaped.

The memorable battle of San Jacinto, April 25, 1836, and the happy results for Texas which followed, will live forever in the hearts of Texas' children. Once again the Texas army, commanded by General Houston, and numbering only 783 men, were in deadly conflict with the Mexican troops (General Cos commanding), who defied the nearly disheartened Texans with a force of upwards of 1500 men. Once again the tide of battle turned against the Texans, when the cry of "*Remember the Alamo!*" rang out above the shrieks of the dying, the clash of artillery, and the tumult of battle. It fired despondent hearts, renewed the courage of faltering ones, and inspired every Texan soldier's arm for deadly blows in vengeance' name. Not one in all that band of dauntless men but had cause to remember the Alamo, and the massacre at Goliad.

With the war-cry of "Remember the Alamo!" surging up from their hearts, and leaping from their lips, they rushed with furious frenzy upon the enemy, and gained a glorious victory, which secured immediately the establishment of the Republic of Texas.

The Last Night.

THEY stand in the shadow which darkly falls
When the Day-god sleeps in his glory,
Shut in by the gloom of the Alamo walls,
Those heroes who live in Fame's story.

Hunters and planters and miners are they,
Giant-builded and iron-hearted,
Unconquered, undaunted, they stand at bay
When their last faint hope has departed.

They are stern of visage and dark of brow,
With a mist in their eyes grown tender,
For memory "troubles the waters" now
In the heart of each brave defender.

There are dear wife hands reaching out to them,
There are sweet childish voices calling;

Love pierces the hearts of these stalwart men
As they stand in the night-shades falling.

The valley is dark with a living host,
The hills with their presence are teeming,
By their camp-fire's glow like a spectral ghost
Each tent through the shadow is gleaming.

With bare, bowed heads in the hush and the gloom
Mid their sad regrets and their sorrow,
They wait for the flush of the "day of doom,"
To crimson these walls on the morrow.

Without are curses that burden the night,
Where the enemy fumes and rages,
Within they are kindling fires to light
Texas homes through all coming ages.

O, thou blood-bought shrine of a nation's pride!
Thou altar of love and of glory!
Thou Alamo! swept by a crimson tide,
Live ever in song and in story!

www.ingramcontent.com/pod-product-compliance
Lightning Source LLC
LaVergne TN
LVHW021425110826
845150LV00007B/2093

* 9 7 8 1 4 2 5 5 0 7 7 9 4 *